T0207877

BORN TO LIVE

CHRIS STORY

BALBOA.PRESS
A DIVISION OF HAY HOUSE

Balboa Press books may be ordered through booksellers or by contacting:

Balboa Press
A Division of Hay House
1663 Liberty Drive
Bloomington, IN 47403
www.balboapress.com
1 (877) 407-4847

Because of the dynamic nature of the Internet, any web addresses or links contained in this book may have changed since publication and may no longer be valid. The views expressed in this work are solely those of the author and do not necessarily reflect the views of the publisher, and the publisher hereby disclaims any responsibility for them.

The author of this book does not dispense medical advice or prescribe the use of any technique as a form of treatment for physical, emotional, or medical problems without the advice of a physician, either directly or indirectly. The intent of the author is only to offer information of a general nature to help you in your quest for emotional and spiritual well-being. In the event you use any of the information in this book for yourself, which is your constitutional right, the author and the publisher assume no responsibility for your actions.

Any people depicted in stock imagery provided by Getty Images are models, and such images are being used for illustrative purposes only. Certain stock imagery © Getty Images.

Print information available on the last page.

ISBN: 978-1-9822-3732-5 (sc)
ISBN: 978-1-9822-3733-2 (e)

Balboa Press rev. date: 10/21/2019

Abraham wet a paper towel, desperately trying to wipe away the mustard stain. Instead of disappearing, it began to spread.

"Oh, come on. Are you kidding me? You just had to stop for that hot dog, didn't you? Dummy," Abe said, louder than he intended.

Just then a toilet flushed behind a closed stall door. A tall, grey-haired man emerged, looked at Abe's situation with a sympathetic smile.

"One of those days, huh?" the stranger said. A comment, not a question.

"Yup. Been a string of 'em," Abe replied without looking up. "Seems like I'd have been better off staying home today."

"Well, who knows, maybe your luck will turn around. They say—"

"You know what?" Abe interrupted, "I really don't care what they, or anyone else has to say right now. No offense, but I'm just not in the mood."

The man dried his hands and quietly left the men's room. Abe continued to work on the stain to no avail.

"Hopeless." He looked in the mirror, not recognizing the worn-out man looking back. *What have I become?*

"How did I end up here?" Abe said to his own reflection. "Well, here goes nothing. Things can't get any worse. This will probably lead to nothing."

Abraham picked his briefcase up off the floor, stood as tall as he could, and took in a deep breath. He marched out of the restroom and rounded the corner to the lobby entrance where he'd come in.

The receptionist looked up and smiled. "Good morning, sir. How may I serve you?"

"Uh, I'm Abraham Finch. I'm supposed to meet Mr. Westport at nine thirty. I'm a few minutes late."

"Yes, sir. I see you on Mr. Westport's calendar. He's in his office expecting you. Let me show you in." The receptionist led Abe to a large wooden door. She pushed it open and gestured for him to go on in. "Good luck," she whispered as he passed by her.

Abe walked into the biggest office he'd ever seen. The room was lined with floor-to-ceiling bookshelves. There was even a ladder on a rail, like you found in old libraries to reach the upper shelves. At the center was a massive mahogany desk with nothing but a telephone on it.

Behind the desk a wall of windows overlooked the park two stories below. A breathtaking view of the mountains beyond. Abe instantly felt out of his league. His stomach tightened.

Just then, at his left, a door concealed in the wall of books opened. In walked a tall grey-haired man. Yes, the very tall, greying man from the restroom. Abe's confidence sank even lower.

The man he'd more or less told off was, in fact, his customer. All the nice man had tried to do was offer some moral support, and Abe had jammed his thumb right into his eye.

"Mr. Westport . . . I didn't—well, I didn't know that you . . . I mean . . ." Abe stammered.

Crossing the room swiftly with his hand outstretched, Mr. Westport put Abe out of his misery. "Don't worry about it, Abraham. Call me Simon."

Abe shook his hand, his heart still in his throat. Barely able to breathe, he said, "Thank you, sir. I'm under a great deal of stress, and . . ." He caught himself midsentence, "Never mind. I'm not here to talk about my problems. I'm here to solve yours."

"Let's see about that." Simon offered Abe a seat. They sat in deep leather chairs facing each other. Abraham thought it strange that Simon wasn't sitting behind his imposing desk.

"Can I offer you a coffee, or tea perhaps?"

Abe thought about his mustard-stained pants and decided against taking any chances with a hot beverage. "No, thank you, sir."

"Simon. Call me Simon, please."

"OK. Simon. Thank you for meeting me today, I know how busy you must be. Again, I'm sorry about before."

"Not to mention it again. Deal?" Simon bargained, pointing his finger at Abe.

Abe smiled. "Deal."

"Now, what problem of mine do you think you have the solution for?" Simon sat back into his chair and put his hands in his lap. He was at complete ease. This made Abe feel more relaxed. He always sold better when he was comfortable.

He went on selling for the next twenty minutes, running at full tilt. Pulled out all the stops. The best pitch of his career. He felt like Babe Ruth pointing his bat into the stands, confident he was about to hit a home run.

After he'd covered all the talking points, answered any possible objections before they could be raised, Abe went in for the close. Absolutely sure he had a deal.

"Simon, are you prepared to start saving money with our products today?"

Simon got up, walked slowly over to his window and gazed at the mountains in the distance. With his back to Abe, he stood silently for an uncomfortably long time.

"Abraham, I like you. You might say that's odd, given the circumstances of our first meeting. But I like you." Turning to face Abe, Simon thrust his hands into his pockets. "But I'm not ready to commit today."

"I don't understand." Abe stood and took a step towards Simon. "What don't you like about our services? I mean, what can I do to make this happen?"

"Son, I hear the desperation in your voice. It's written all over your face." Simon walked to Abe and put his hand on his shoulder. "Honestly, I want to help you. But I'm not ready to say yes today. It's not personal. I simply need time to think this over, and consult with my team. I'm not saying no, just not yet."

Abe sat back down and stared at the floor. He'd hit rock bottom. Instantly his mind flashed to the mortgage statement tucked into his briefcase. Three months behind, and now they were going to start foreclosure if he didn't make a payment very soon.

He hadn't closed a sale in nearly four months, and they'd run through what little savings they had to keep the lights on, car payments made, and food on the table. He hadn't told his wife how bad things were. Samantha was six months pregnant—the last thing she needed was this kind of stress.

"Abe, I've been right where you are. Or at least where I think you are. Son, I'm here to tell you it will pass. You'll get through this. What I was going to tell you back there in the bathroom was, every adversity comes with the seed of an equivalent or greater benefit," Simon said. He walked back to the window and gazed at the view. He continued, "Those aren't my words, they belong to Napoleon Hill. Ever heard of him?"

Abe looked up. "No."

"Abe, when I was down—I mean down and nearly out—I thought my life was over. I even thought about taking my own life, to tell you the truth. Then I read those words by Mr. Hill. At first, I didn't believe them. Sounded like a bunch of nonsense.

"But the more I thought about it, the more sense it made. In every circumstance of my life, up to that point, when faced with a challenge I overcame it. Not only had I overcome, but I'd been better off for having gone through it." Simon turned back to Abe.

"Yeah. Tell me—tell me what good is going to come from me losing my house? What good will come from my pregnant wife being out on the streets?" Abe was angry, his words came as a fear-laced torrent.

"I don't know, Abe. And neither do you. But one thing I do know, is if you accept that you have within you the ability to overcome, then you will. Not only will you overcome, you'll end up in a much better place than you could have imagined." Simon smiled as he spoke. He had a distant look in his eyes, as if he were thinking back on a fond memory.

"I offered you my best. You know what I'm selling will be good for your company. Why don't you just say yes?" Abe's eyes were watering. He couldn't believe his own ears. *What on earth am I doing? I'm reduced to begging?*

"Abraham," Simon's eyes narrowed. "You have not offered me your best. Nor have you given your best. You came here not to serve me, but to serve yourself. You came here wanting to solve your own problems, not mine."

"But—that's not true. Honestly, it's not," Abe said, near whimpering.

"I want you to go and think about what I've shared with you today. You need to look within, and look for the seed of benefit that's waiting for you."

Simon escorted Abe to the door and closed it behind him.

He stood outside Simon's door for a couple of minutes. Debating whether he should just leave, or march back in there and not take no for an answer.

"Forget it. It's no use." he muttered to himself.

He walked back through the lobby with his head down and shoulders slumped. The receptionist was not a body language expert, but she knew this unlucky salesman with mustard on his pants had been rejected.

"Have a nice day, sir."

Abe walked on past her without a word. She smiled sympathetically.

A steady snow had started falling while Abe was in his meeting with Simon. Large flakes were coming down in no particular hurry. Abe used his arm to clear the snow from the driver's side door, flung his briefcase inside, and fell into the seat. He slammed the door and screamed. A guttural noise that seemed to start all the way down in his toes and work its way through his entire body and out his mouth.

"Why? Why, God? Why have you abandoned me?" he shouted while beating his steering wheel.

He put his head on the wheel and sobbed. He cried until he had nothing left. He couldn't remember the last time he'd cried. Maybe when his mother died. But even then he'd kept his composure for his father's sake.

"I'm done. There's nothing I can do. We're going to lose everything."

Abe sat up, suddenly aware that he was having a tantrum in a public parking lot. He stuck the key in the ignition, started the motor, shifted the car into gear, and drove off.

Unable to process what had gone wrong, Abe raced from point to point in his mind. It really was the best presentation he'd ever given, he was sure of it. *Mr. Westport said no because of what happened in the bathroom. That's the only thing that makes any sense.*

"I can't believe I lost a sale over a hot dog," he snapped at his reflection in the rearview mirror.

He drove fast, too fast for the road conditions. Abe wanted to get out of town, get away from everyone for a while. He needed to figure out a solution to this whole mess.

"How will I tell Samantha? She's going to freak out. This isn't the way our life was supposed to go!" he yelled at himself.

Taking a sharp left turn, the car skidded on the slick snow. The momentary loss of control brought Abe back to attention. He gripped the steering wheel with both hands and sat upright.

He took the old road out of town, heading south towards a small fishing village called Hope. Abe smiled at the irony. Here he was hopeless, and headed to a place actually called Hope. A tiny spec on the map with a few hundred year-round residents. Hope had a post office that doubled as a café, a boat harbor lined with gifts shops, and quaint B&Bs.

Abe and Sam liked coming to Hope for long weekend getaways. There was a peaceful nature to Hope you couldn't describe. You had to feel it, you had to experience it to understand. Some places in the world had an energy that replenished your soul. Hope was one of those places.

Mindlessly, Abe drove on through the snow building up on the road. The storm had gotten worse since he left Simon's office. Flurries of snow were now whipping across the road with gusts of wind, at times making it impossible to see.

By the time conditions neared whiteout, Abe realized he was closer to Hope than to home. Might as well press on and wait this storm out at the café.

He slowed to a crawl, barely able to see fifty feet in front of his car. His heart was beating fast—this was a bad decision. He shouldn't be on the road.

He scolded himself. "Just chalk it up to yet another stupid thing you've done. Seems that's my expertise lately. Stupid."

Rounding a sharp corner, Abe picked up a little speed. The wind had died down some and he could see far enough ahead to make up for some lost time. His phone buzzed. He reached into his coat pocket—it wasn't there. It kept buzzing. He tried the other pocket. Not there either. Then he remembered shoving it into his briefcase.

He leaned over and opened the case, snatching up the phone. Eyes back on the road, then to the phone. It was Sam. She'd be wondering where he was. He'd promised to call her when he was out of his appointment. Sam had wanted to discuss paint colors for the nursery.

He put the unanswered phone down on the passenger seat. He looked up just in time to see a figure in the middle of the road. A man, come out of nowhere. Abe slammed on the brakes, turned the wheel, and went into an uncontrollable spin. The world was going round and round in a white blur. The car finally came to a sudden stop. Abe lurched forward, slamming against his seatbelt so hard he blacked out.

Abe could feel a pain in his shoulder where the seat belt had stopped him from flying into the windshield. Barely aware of what had happened, he felt pieces of memories before the blackout coming back to him. It had been snowing. There was a man in the road.

He opened his eyes suddenly and looked around. The snow had stopped falling. It was brighter than before. He could see the road in both directions. His car was so close to the bluff on the driver's side he could look over the edge to the deep canyon below.

"Oh, Lord. Thank you . . . thank you," Abe rejoiced.

The engine had stopped at some point. He put it in park and switched off the ignition. Turned the key and it roared to life. "Thank you, God."

Abe wasn't one to pray, but these were extraordinary circumstances. He had forgotten all about his present financial worries. They'd been replaced by a sudden rush of joy to be alive. He thought about that fact for a moment. He smiled. Then remembered the man in the road.

He was nowhere to be seen now. Panic and dread took hold of Abe. Had he killed the man? He put the car in gear and tried to move forward. The tires spun, the car didn't budge.

He threw it into reverse and again the tires spun free, like he was parked on ball bearings. Abe craned his neck in all directions. No sign of anyone, anywhere. His phone had fallen to the floor, and he bent down to reach for it. Straining, he grabbed it up, and pain shot through his entire body. He figured he must have hit against his seat belt harder than he thought.

1 Missed Call

That was Sam's call. He wished he'd answered it. No signal. Not even one bar. Maybe if he got out he could find a spot with service. He opened his door, but he could get it open only a crack before it came hard against a snow berm. He looked out and remembered the canyon edge less than a foot away. Maybe the other side was safer anyway.

Before he could maneuver over, the passenger door opened. The man who'd been standing in the road stooped down and poked his head in.

"Mind if I join you?" the stranger said. His eyes were bright green and smiling. Wild strands of grey hair stuck out from under his red fedora. His wrinkled face was familiar, but Abe was sure they'd never met.

"Of course. Are you all right?"

"Never better, friend. Never better." He squeezed himself into the seat and shut the door. The stranger lifted Abe's briefcase and put it in the backseat. "Businessman, huh?"

"Yes. Well, sort of. I'm in sales. Of course, I haven't made any lately." Abe scolded himself for whining to a perfect stranger. "What are you doing out here in the middle of this storm anyway?"

"One could ask the same of you, friend."

"I was on my way to Hope. Needed a drive. I didn't expect the storm to pick up like it did," Abe explained.

"I'm on my way to Hope too. How about I tag along?"

Abe looked at him, "I'm stuck, sir. I'm sorry, not able to move an inch."

"Sounds like song lyrics, huh? Stuck on my way to Hope." The stranger laughed at his own joke.

Abe thought it was funny too. "Yeah, maybe a country song. Only we don't have any beer."

They both laughed out loud.

"Let me get out and take a gander at how badly you're stuck. Maybe you just need a push in the right direction." The old man slipped out of the seat into the now bright blue-sky day.

Abe felt stupid just sitting there, but he was stuck, after all. Maybe the old guy was right, he just needed a push in the right direction.

Abe watched in the rearview mirror as his new friend appraised the situation. Then he turned his head to follow him around to the front. The stranger grimaced and shook his head.

Getting back in, the old man said, "Ain't going anywhere, son. We are stuck good."

"Think we can dig a little? Maybe free up a little space to get a run at it?" Abe asked.

"Nope. You're buried past the axles. It's hard packed too. Stuck like nobody's business."

Abe felt a sudden sense of panic. His heart started to race. Almost on cue, the old man put his hand on Abe's shoulder and said, "Relax, son. We are going to be OK. Take a deep breath . . . just slow down."

"My wife, Sam, she's going to worry. She doesn't know where I am. I never told her I was going to Hope. She tried to call. I ignored it." Abe's eyes were watering, and a single tear spilled out and rolled down his cheek.

"My name is Eugene. Eugene Duncan. Friends call me Gene." The old man stretched out his hand.

Abe took it and they shook. "Nice to meet you, Gene. I'm Abraham Finch. I nearly killed you. Why were you standing in the road anyway?"

"You know, if I hadn't been standing where I was, you would have driven right off the cliff."

Abe looked out the window, imagining plummeting down the thousand feet or more to the bottom. He shivered. "I guess it's lucky for me you were there. But why are you walking? Where do you live?"

Gene looked straight ahead, "Abraham, I walk to clear my head. Gather my thoughts. You know, on these walks I meet the most interesting people in the world. Like you. If I hadn't been out walking, I would never have met you."

"I'm sorry, Gene. I'm afraid you won't find me interesting. In fact, to the contrary. My life is a total mess. There is nothing interesting about me. Trust me."

"Abraham, I already know that isn't true. First off, you're a businessman. A salesman. That's one of the most fascinating careers on planet earth." Gene's eyes were smiling as he spoke. He was being sincere.

"I'm not sure I agree with you on that point. Truth is, I'm not even sure I've got a career. Gene, it's been months since I've closed a deal. I'm near losing my house. I'm not so sure things wouldn't have been better if I'd plunged over the cliff. I mean, at least my wife would be taken care of. See, I have a decent policy."

Gene sat back in his seat. He looked ahead and closed his eyes. Worried he'd offended him, Abe said, "I'm sorry. You don't need to hear my problems."

Gene looked back to Abe and said, "Abraham, I've been right where you are. I have looked into that very canyon. I too have wondered if I would be better off, if the world would be better off with me at the bottom of it."

Abe didn't know what to say. For so long he had felt alone. Like no one would understand. No one could possibly understand or relate to what he was going through.

"Abraham, may I tell you a story?"

"Looks like we aren't going anywhere for a while. Let me have it." Abe faked a half smile.

"I had just turned thirty-two. My wife had thrown a big bash in my honor. She pulled out all the stops. Invited all my friends and colleagues. She even hired a four-piece band and rented out a banquet hall.

"Money was no object. We had plenty. She spared no expense. The best wine and food. The works. You want to know who was the last to arrive at my party?"

Abe looked back to Gene. "I'm guessing you."

"Good guess. But I wasn't just late, I nearly missed it. The band was packing up their instruments when I arrived. About half of the guests had already left. But there was my wife, entertaining people she barely knew, and could have cared less for.

"When I stepped into the hall, our eyes met. I felt horrible. She looked spectacular. Radiant. I saw love in her eyes. But her face couldn't mask the disappointment in her heart. This wasn't the first promise I'd broken.

"Most nights she and our two little girls ate dinner by themselves. Wondering when Daddy was coming home. My workday ended most nights long after they'd already been tucked in.

"And you know what, Abraham? I told them I was doing it for them. All the hard work, the nights and weekends at the office, all of it for them. So they could have a better life than I'd had. They'd want for nothing in this world. Nothing except for me.

"I was the only one who believed my story of self-sacrifice. My woe is me story fell on deaf ears. Missing my own birthday party was just another in a long string of letdowns. My wife had grown accustomed to being disappointed.

"Seeing the pain I'd caused that night hit me hard. I made one more promise. I promised to never miss another family event again. Ever. No matter what, I swore I'd make time to be there . . . no matter what."

Gene looked down at his hands folded in his lap. He paused for a long moment, then looked back to Abe, smiling widely. "I meant it too. You have to know that.

It's important that you know I meant to keep that promise. And for a while I did.

"I was home for dinner three to four nights a week. Saturday mornings I stayed home. Even made pancakes a couple of times. My girls were loving the extra time with Daddy. To be honest, I'd never been happier.

"Then something happened. We lost a couple of major clients, key accounts that were very lucrative to my firm. They just walked out the door taking their money with them.

"I snapped. Our company could have survived the hit. In my mind though, Abe . . . this was the signaling of the end. I mean, this looked like the start of a downward spiral." Gene looked at Abe. He gave him a crooked smile. "You know what bothered me most, Abe?"

"What?"

"Losing. I hated to lose. Not just the money. I had plenty, and we could have easily weathered the loss of a couple of accounts. The real reason I snapped, the truth was, I simply despised losing."

Abe turned to Gene, "What'd you do? Did you get the accounts back?"

"I thought you might ask that very question."

"What do you mean?"

"You remind me of myself, Abe. And that's the exact thing I would have wanted to know. Did I get the business back? Or put another way, did I win?"

"OK. Yeah—did you win? Did you win back the business?"

"Abe, I'm going to answer your question. But first let me tell you more of the story."

Abe looked at his watch, then up and down the road. He hoped a car would come along and pull him out any minute.

"Am I keeping you?" Gene asked, having noticed Abe glancing at his watch.

"Oh no. Just don't want to spend the night out here. Yes, please tell me the story," Abe said.

"I was at home on a Saturday morning, like I said, I was making pancakes for my girls. The phone rang. It was my associate director of sales. He told me about the two major clients jumping ship.

"I dropped everything and raced to the office. Leaving my family to finish making breakfast without me. They'd go on to eat it without me, too.

"I spent the rest of the day and most of Sunday working on a proposal to get my customers back. Yes. I did get them back. In fact, the campaign we developed over the weekend was so effective, we ended up increasing sales across the board for the next two quarters in a row.

"Have you heard the expression, with every adversity there is a seed of an equivalent or greater benefit?"

"Yes. That's weird. I just heard that this morning for the first time."

"Well, it's true. We were hitting it out of the park after nearly losing some major clients. It was fantastic. I was on cloud nine. My family understood. They were disappointed but not surprised."

"Gene, you and I have the exact opposite problem. I'm not knocking it out of the park. I'm behind on all my payments and promises. You at least were killing it financially. I'd trade almost everything for that right now. Do you know the stress I'm under? My wife and I are expecting. Gene, we may not have a place to bring our baby home to. You missed some pancakes, no offense, but big deal."

Gene had a faraway look in his eyes. He smiled to himself.

"Abraham, you are right. I was killing it. Money came easily. But there comes a time in life when you realize that all the money in the world won't buy the one thing you really want. The one thing you need more than anything. When you reach that moment of understanding, you just hope it isn't too late."

"Too late for what?" Abe asked.

"Too late to make a difference. You see, my story doesn't end with winning back my customers. Want to hear the rest?"

"Yeah," Abe replied without looking at Gene.

"After that Saturday morning, I started spending even more time at the office. Like I said, the new system we developed was so effective our sales were growing by leaps and bounds.

"I'd set new targets and goals. Reaching higher and higher up the ladder, I was projecting profits beyond any previous expectation. I wanted to break all records and set the bar so high, no one could touch us.

"One early morning on my way out the door, my wife stopped me. She was standing at the top of the stairs looking down at me. My hand on the doorknob, leaving before anyone in the house was up.

"She asked if I'd be able to come to the girls' dance recital that night. 'It starts at six,' she said. She wanted us all to go together as a family. It would mean the world to the girls if I'd come home in time to take them all."

Gene's voice lowered as he continued his story. Abe found himself leaning in closer.

"You can probably imagine how my day went. In and out of meetings, both with my team and customers. Every hour was occupied with moving towards my new bigger, better goals. I was so consumed with my own success, I didn't stop for lunch. As long as my coffee cup was full, I kept moving through the day.

"Next thing I knew, it was quarter to six. I grabbed the phone, dialed home. My wife answered on the first ring. Not happy. I explained that my day had exploded. She was used to that. I told her to go on ahead without me, promising to be there before they danced. She had heard too many promises for too long. She hung up without another word.

"I felt horrible. I grabbed my hat and coat and raced to the elevator. By the time I got to the school, the recital was well underway. I took a seat at the back. I might not be sitting with my wife, but at least I made it. After the last solo dancer had performed, all the little girls in their variety of colorful tutus came out for a final on-stage bow and twirl, then the curtain fell.

"But neither of my girls were on the stage. I was confused. Were they in the back and didn't know to come out? I got to my feet and followed the pack into the lobby area. I stood near the door waiting for my wife to emerge. She didn't. I asked around—no one had seen her. The dance instructor said they'd never showed.

"My heart was beating a hundred miles per hour, blood pounding in my ears. The world fell silent. Imagining the very worst, I was screaming inwardly. 'How could you miss this? You promised!' But what if—what if something bad had happened?"

Abe was visibly shaken. His mind had leapt to the worst conclusion too. "What happened, Gene? Where were they?"

"Abraham, I'm telling you this story not for your sympathy—rather, in sympathy for where you're at in life. Please understand this isn't easy to share, but I'm willing to tell you my story in hopes that I can help you avoid the pitfalls that destroyed my life.

"You asked where they were? I'll tell you. But you have to promise me something first. OK?"

"Sure. OK. Promise you what?"

"Abraham, I need you to promise me that you'll keep an open mind throughout my entire story. Even if what I'm about to tell you seems strange or impossible. OK?"

Abe thought for a moment, wondering who this guy actually was. He had never explained what he was doing out here in the storm.

"Promise?" Gene asked.

"Yes. I promise."

"I called home twice. No answer. I left the school speeding for the house. Hoping my greatest fears were for nothing. Praying that they simply hadn't been able to get the car started. My wife was famous for running on fumes. Maybe she'd run out of gas and was stranded on the side of the road. Perhaps she was waiting for her knight in shining armor to come along and rescue her.

I am that knight, I swore to myself. I promised God that if He'd let me find them safe and sound, I'd never take them for granted again. I'd honor and cherish my family every day. For the rest of my life. Oh please, God, let them be safe.

I prayed and prayed for the seven miles to the house. They weren't there, and no sign of them on the road there."

Gene looked off into the distance. His eyes began to water, confirming the ending that Abe had foreseen. Abe could see him reliving that moment in his mind.

"No one was home. But lying there on the floor in the entryway was a small rag doll. My youngest girl never left home without it. She was attached to that little doll. She called it Mindy, and Mindy went everywhere with her. Everywhere. She must have dropped it in the rush to get out the door when I didn't show up.

"I scooped Mindy up off the floor and held her tight. Tears ran freely down my face and landed on the doll. I put it in my coat pocket and ran back to my idling car. As I stepped back out into the night, hope was alive somewhere in my mind. A state of denial took ahold of me. They were out there waiting for me. I'd find them. I had to."

Abe was near tears, on the verge of being a father himself, he was wracked with emotions for Gene's wife and little girls.

"Well?" Abe prompted. "Where were they? Where'd you find them?"

"Abraham, listen to me. This is my story. Just listen." Gene sat back into his seat and looked out towards the canyon. "The roads were wet that night. My wife was a good enough driver. But she was angry, in a hurry, and it was dark.

"I drove back towards the school, exactly as she would have. A couple of miles from the house I saw the flashing lights of an ambulance and two police cars. An officer directing traffic motioned me to stop. I rolled down my window. He said to keep moving slowly, and stay left.

"I asked what had happened, not wanting to hear the answer. He said a car had gone over the edge. I shut the car off and got out. The cop was talking to me, but I didn't hear a word he said. I raced to the edge of the embankment, my stomach aching with pain like I'd been kicked by a horse. My eyes confirmed what my heart already knew—it was my wife's car.

"The cop grabbed my shoulders, spun me around. He was yelling something, then the big man in uniform froze when he saw my face. He put his arm around me and walked with me to the ambulance. Three bodies were laid out on the road under a cover. One adult, and two small figures draped in blankets.

"I dropped to my knees and screamed into the night sky. I started crawling towards them, but the cop pulled me to my feet and directed me to the ambulance. It took two of them to hold me back.

"They sedated me with something, I didn't wake up for I don't know how many hours. Abraham, when I came to, I relived the tragedy all over again. The pain was too much. I wanted to die."

Abe sat up straight in his seat. He avoided eye contact with Gene and stared ahead. He felt a sudden sense of embarrassment for how he'd portrayed his own circumstance as so dire. What Gene had been through was unimaginable.

"Gene, I'm so sorry," Abe said barely above a whisper.

"I went back the next day. I had to see. Nothing seemed real, but there it was. Her car. Crumpled like a pop can at the bottom of the ravine. I wanted to join them. You know, I had a pistol in my pocket. My plan was to end it, right then and there.

"I felt the cold steel of the gun. I wrapped my fingers around it. Gripping it tight. This was all my fault. If I'd come home on time none of this would have happened. My wife would be alive. My little girls would be alive. It was me. I'd killed them."

Gene looked at Abe for an uncomfortable moment, then turned back to the window.

Abe wanted to know more, but he didn't want to pry. This wasn't an easy subject to broach. "Gene, are you OK?"

"You're a good man, Abraham. You are. Yes, I'm OK. You are probably wondering why I didn't take my own life that day."

"I mean, I'm glad you didn't—but yeah. What happened?"

"I pulled the gun from my pocket and looked around, no cars coming. As I lifted the gun to my head, something caught my attention out of the corner of my eye.

"As if materializing from thin air, a man was walking towards me. I quickly concealed the pistol back in my pocket. As I turned to face the stranger approaching, I saw he wore a long, tattered trench coat. His face was dirty, his beard a tangled mess. His narrow eyes held a cold and faraway look. Like he was there, but also somewhere else.

"'Pardon me, sir. Don't mean to interrupt. Have you a couple of bucks you could part with? I'm in need of something to eat.'

"Clearly, he was. No exaggeration there. He was rail thin; his face, although concealed by his shabby beard, was hollow.

"I let go of the pistol in my coat pocket, and reached into my pants for my wallet. Mindlessly I opened it, retrieved all the cash within and stretched out my hand towards him.

"'That's too much, sir. Maybe just one of them. That'll do.'

"I looked at my hand, I was holding four one-hundred-dollar bills. Crisp. Bright green and straight as arrows. The very sight of them made me sick. 'Take them,' I said. 'I have no need of money. Take them.'

"'Why, thank you, sir. I'll spend this wisely.'

"He folded the bills and stuffed them into a small pocket in the front of his coat. Carefully he buttoned it up tight. Then he patted the pocket with its precious content.

"'I wasn't always like this, you know?' he said. 'No sir. I used to have a fine home, cars, and plenty of money.'

"'What happened?' I asked, even though I wasn't in the mood for a story. Something compelled me to ask. I had to know.

"'Life. You see, life, it was so much better back then. That was before everything fell apart. I used to be respected in my community. I was an artist. I made fine paintings. Each piece was sold before my canvas had time to dry. My work was in great demand. My art was displayed in the best homes of the best people. The fancy folks, oh, they clamored to be at my openings at the galleries. They wanted to see me, and be seen with me.'

"I found myself enchanted with this washed-up shell of a man. 'What happened?' I heard myself asking.

"'Life was better then. People had good taste. They appreciated me and my work. They understood it. But then they changed. Before I knew what had happened, I was out. Out of style, is what my agent said. Paint what they want these days, he said. They want brighter, more lively work. Well, I refused. My work was good the way it was. They'd come back to me, I kept thinking. I was sure of it. But you know what? They never did. Life moved on past me. It gave me the boot, and I lost everything. Back in the day though, I had it all.'

"I looked at this pathetic wretch of a man for a long quiet moment. What could you say to someone who had lost so much? Then it struck me like a bolt of lightning. I was someone who'd just lost it all. Sure, I had money, plenty of it. But I would have traded every dime of it to have my family back. To hold my little girls one more time.

"I realized in that moment that I was looking at myself. This man, the washed-up shell of a man, was me. He'd given up on life, just as I was about to do." Gene closed his eyes and held a deep breath, then slowly exhaled and turned to face Abe.

"Did you ever see the artist again?" Abe asked.

"No, I never did. But his spirit has stayed with me ever since that day," Gene replied.

Abe and Gene sat silently in the car for a while. Abe tried to figure out what kept a man going when he'd faced the tragedy of losing his family. How could you go on with life when you believed you were responsible for the death of your entire family?

"Gene, what do you mean the artist's spirit has been with you?" Abe asked.

"He has become a spiritual advisor."

"What? A spiritual advisor? How's that?" Abe was very confused.

Gene smiled wide, loving that he'd captured Abe's attention. "The artist comes to me from time to time. When I need his wisdom most."

"He didn't seem all that wise to me. Seems more like a loser. A loser who can't get over the way things used to be," Abe observed.

"I won't argue with you on that point, Abraham. You hit the nail on the head. Indeed, his best years were behind him. The memories of his glory days were all he had left. He could have moved on with his work, created paintings for the market. Instead, he just quit. Quit moving forward and lived completely in the past. When life was good. He was as stuck in the past, Abraham, as you are stuck here on the side of the road.

"He couldn't move an inch further down the road of life. When I catch myself making decisions based on how things used to be, the artist comes to me. He encourages me to stay right there in the past. He reminds me of how good those days were. With a blinding light he illuminates the way backwards to the past.

"I thank him for coming along. I reach into my wallet, hand him a few more bucks, and off he goes. That is how he has become my spiritual advisor. He is a stalwart reminder of the dangers of living one's life immersed in the past."

Abe said, "But if you ignore the past, aren't you doomed to repeat it?"

"Quite right, Abraham. Learn from the past, but don't live your entire life there. Those days are gone. Visit them from time to time, and enjoy the glow of fond memories, or the lessons taught from mistakes made. If you intend to live your life in the past, then you'll be doomed to the fate of the artist. Wandering the back roads of life with no future, no hope, and no purpose."

Abe put his head down, "I used to close deals constantly. Sales just came naturally. Money wasn't an issue at all. We had plenty. Clients were happy to say yes. They wanted to buy. Now, I can't sell anything. And it does feel like my life depends on it.

"I find myself thinking about the old days a lot lately. Like, I just want it to be that way again. I'm using all my same techniques, but nothing's working. Maybe I'm just like that artist, spending too much time in the past."

Gene put his hand on Abe's shoulder, "Use the past, use the successes from those days as lessons. What can you learn from them? Stay in the past only long enough to learn the important lesson, then snap out of it. Stay too long, and you're right—you'll end up just like the artist. Living in the shadow of a life that once was, and will never be again."

Abe looked out over the canyon, thinking about Samantha. He shuddered at the thought of how close he'd come to going over the edge. A tingling sensation traveled up and down his spine as he imagined her giving birth to their child, alone.

"Abraham!" Gene hollered.

"What?" Abe said as he turned back to Gene.

"Stay with me."

"I'm right here. I'm stuck, not going anywhere." His voice held more than a little sarcasm.

"Abraham, you were wondering how I could go on. How could I go on living, while knowing in my heart that I was responsible for the death of my family. Right?"

"Well, yes. I don't mean to offend. It's just—"

"No offense taken. You are right to wonder. As you now know, I was wondering too. After all, I'd gone to the road side to end it all. Hadn't I? That would have put me out of my own suffering."

"But then the artist came along."

"Yes. He left me standing there by the side of the road, certain that going backwards is no way forward. But my family was still gone. I was still alone and in pain. How could I go on? How on earth could I live a life with this heavy burden?

"As I stood there, fingering the gun in my pocket, and trying to build the courage to do what I'd come there to do, I heard footsteps. I turned, expecting to see the artist once more. But it wasn't him. It was a well-dressed young man. Much younger than the artist. Younger than I. I guessed him to be twenty-four.

"Tall, a good-looking guy. Clean shaven and well dressed. He tipped his cap to me and said, 'Howdy. Hope I'm not interrupting something.'

"I said, 'No. I'm just standing here. What are you doing out here?'

"'I'm working out a problem. See, I'm a writer. When I get blocked, I go on long walks to clear my head and look for inspiration. Nothing worse than being stuck in front of a blank page with an empty head.'

"'I guess,' I replied. Knowing damn well that what I was going through was far worse than any problem writers block presented.

"He went on, 'One day, I'm going to be published. Then, I'm going to have everything. First, I think I'll get a place in the city. I like to be in the city on weekends. Then I'll get a place in the country, where I can be alone and write. Get away from it all.

"'You know what I mean? Somewhere that the air is fresh. I might even get some animals. That is, if my wife would like some. I'm not married yet, but when I'm published, and my books are selling, I plan to meet a woman.

"'I want to have several books out by then. Then I'm going to probably take some time off. We might even go sailing in the South Pacific. No—I don't know how to sail. But I'm going to learn. I've always wanted to. One day I will, when my book is published.'

"Distracted once again from my own troubles, I asked how far along his book was.

"'Oh, I'm in the developmental stages right now. Have been for the last couple years. But I've read that plenty of authors do that. Think, ponder, and plan. Then the stories burst onto the page with abandon. That's my plan. See, when my books are out there, and people know my name, then I'm going to put out one a year.

"'That's the way I will do it, once I get the first one published.'

"I don't know much about the publishing world or the business of the literary. But it seemed to me this guy was missing the boat. I asked, 'Are you submitting any work to magazines? Like short stories or essays?'

"He didn't like that. He wrinkled his nose and shook his head. 'No way. There's no money in that any more. Nope, that's not the future of publishing. No, I want to have full-length novels with my name on them. You know, when I sell enough, I might even get approached by movie producers. Can you imagine? I can't wait to see my own story up on the big screen.'

"I looked at the young man with pity. He was basing his entire happiness on what might happen in the future. The businessman in me came to life. I asked him what his immediate goals were for getting his work out there to the public, if not through short stories, then what?

"'You know, for now I don't want to unveil any of my work. Once I have my manuscript complete, then I will find just the right agent who appreciates my work. From there, the sky's the limit. Goals, you say? I'm not some salesman hawking my wares. Please, I'm an author. When I'm published it will all come together for me.'

"I looked back into the depths of the ravine. It occurred to me this young man was living his entire life in the future. I was pretty sure he didn't have one. He saw nothing in front of him in this moment. Everywhere he looked, he saw the glow of tomorrow. A better, brighter day ahead. He could see at the horizon's edge his pot of gold.

"The only problem was, he was never going to get there. He would keep chasing the sunset and missing it by mere moments. The illusion of his destiny lived on the winds of a time not yet born, with no foothold on the path that leads to real happiness."

"Real happiness," said Abe. "There's a mythical creature. To be honest, Gene, I'm not sure there is such a thing as *real happiness.*"

"Abraham, you might be right. One thing I can tell you for sure, if tomorrow is where you live, today will never hold happiness. The young author walked away from me towards an unknown future that he preferred to the reality of his present life.

"I was pretty sure he'd spend the rest of his days walking, waiting, and wanting. Waiting for his moment to shine, and wanting unearned treasure. Until you are willing to pay the price, with your time and initiative, the pot of gold you seek will always be one step ahead of you."

Abe sat still for a while, enjoying the silence between them. He wondered what that author ever ended up accomplishing, if anything at all. He then turned his thoughts inward once more. Back to his current position, stuck in his car, and stuck in his life. At least the author had something to look forward to.

As if he read Abe's mind, Gene said, "And that's all he'll ever have, something to look forward to."

Abe had lost track of time, enjoying the company of the strange old man. His story had successfully distracted him from the fact that they'd been stuck in the car for several hours. The sun was still high in the sky, the brightest day Abe could remember for some time.

"Gene, I guess I understand the whole thing about not living in the future, like the author. And well, yeah, not living only in the past either, like the painter. But what I don't get, and don't be offended—"

"Abraham, I haven't let anyone offend me in over thirty years. Shoot straight."

"I just don't get how you were able to move on. I mean, that's what I don't understand. Like, all you had was the memories of your family. How'd you get through? Where was the benefit? What did you end up doing?" Abe spoke with an urgency he hadn't intended.

Gene was quiet for a moment, then smiled. He turned to Abe and said, "Son, I want to tell you about a little girl I met. After the author walked away, I stood there for a long time. Just me, my gun, and my desperate thoughts. Thoughts like you just described—what was the point of going on? How could I live with myself? What use was there in facing this moment? Why not just end it all?

"A small voice disturbed my wicked thoughts. Coming towards me was a young girl. She wore a stocking cap down low to her ears, and a frilly white dress. She spun and twirled as she walked. She was singing; her voice was angelic.

"Tears filled my eyes. I saw in her my little girls. The dances I'd missed over the years, and all the life I'd never have with them. I dropped to my knees and doubled over in pain, weeping like a child. The little girl ran to me.

"She put her arms around my shoulders and whispered in my ear, 'It's OK. It's all going to be OK.'

"I looked up into her big round eyes, filled with life and hope. She was bright and had an energy that glowed. She was angelic. There was a softness about her. Her face was frail, and her little body was thin. She pulled back and began to sing again. A joyful version of 'Amazing Grace.' There I knelt before her on the gravel road. Her voice was soothing, and strong for her age. I dried my eyes and felt a slight smile crawling over my face. She was my guardian angel, no doubt about it. Heaven sent, of that I was sure.

"As she sang the final note of the song, I realized at some point I'd closed my eyes. My girls and my wife had been dancing before me in my mind. As if they were really there with me. I felt their presence.

"I opened my eyes half expecting to see my family. The little girl was still standing there. I looked around—just the two of us.

"'You are in pain,' she said.

"'Yes. I am.'

"She gazed deep into my eyes, as if she could see through me. When I looked back, really looked back, I saw into her soul. We shared a connection that I can't explain in words.

"But what I saw was pure joy. Nothing but joy. I am not sure how I knew, but I absolutely knew that she was filled with joy.

"A happiness I hadn't known for a very long time, perhaps since I was a kid. When you are young, you live in the moment. The future is a lifetime away, you simply put one foot in front of the other and let today be your entire world.

"But then something happens. You become aware of time, mortality, and a sense of urgency takes over. At least that's what happened to me. That urgency, the desire to win more, get more, and be more is what killed my family, and what was killing me that day.

"The little girl began to dance and twirl, she spun and leapt to music only she could hear. I found myself smiling again. Her joy was contagious. Inspiring. She made me forget about my own pain, the pain that had brought me to the edge of the ravine. The pain that had me standing at the brink of life ready to call it quits.

"As she spun around, her hat fell off. She kept on dancing and twirling. I bent over to pick it up, and that's when I noticed. She was completely bald. Her smooth head flung back as she whirled around and around.

I looked down at the hat, then back to the little girl who was showing me how to live. Even all the while, it appeared she was dying."

Abe had lost all track of time. He looked at Gene and locked eyes, waiting for him to continue. Abe released a breath he didn't realize he had been holding. It hurt to breathe in and out. He figured the seatbelt was bothering him. He reached to take it off, but Gene grabbed his hand.

"Abe, stay with me. I'm not done with my story."

"OK. I'm right here. What was wrong with her? Did she have cancer?" Abe asked, prompting Gene back to his story.

"I watched her dancing there on that quiet gravel road. Feeling sorry for her. She was fighting something—I assumed cancer. Handing her the small knit hat, I noticed a name was stitched on the inside. Gabrielle. What a beautiful name, I thought.

"She skipped over to me, and took the hat. She put it back on her head and smiled. I smiled back. Gone was any pity I had for her, replaced by that sense of joy. I wasn't sure where it was coming from. I had no reason to feel joyful, my life was a total disaster. My family taken from me and I blamed myself.

"Why on earth would I have any feeling of joy or happiness? I didn't deserve it. And yet, here I was smiling at Gabrielle.

"'Mister, what's your name?' she asked.

"'I'm Eugene . . . but call me Gene. You have a wonderful voice, and you dance like an angel.'

"'My momma says I am an angel, from Heaven. She says that's why I have to go back, soon.'

"I felt a knot in my stomach. This young lady knew she wasn't long for this life. Her place wasn't here on earth, but in Heaven.

"Abe, we all know we aren't going to live forever. But here she was, staring the ultimate truth of life and death right in the face, and still she was joyful. Not an ounce of sorrow or sadness in her being."

Abe was looking again into the deep canyon, remembering how he had imagined having driven over. How it would have solved his financial problems with the life insurance. Suddenly aware of the quiet, Abe glanced back at Gene, who was staring at him intently.

"Sorry. I was lost in thought. Go on . . . I want to hear more about Gabrielle."

"I asked her where her parents were. Why was she out here all alone? I'll never forget her answer. I can feel the hair on the back of my neck stand up as I think about it even now.

"She said, 'I'm never alone.' It wasn't just what she said, it was how she said it. Gabrielle's voice held a confidence beyond her years. Absent were any doubt or insecurities. How could such a young girl have so much assurance and peace about her?

"I wanted to ask about her sickness, but the words escaped me. She could see it on my face. 'I've got leukemia. But it doesn't have me,' she said as she twirled and gave a curtsy.

"'I'm so sorry,' I said.

"She looked up at me, and put her hand out. I took it. She was frail.

"'Don't be sorry for me. I'm not. I'm alive. I'm here, right here. Right now.'

"I looked at her with my mouth gaping. Not sure if she understood what she was actually dealing with. Did she not realize the peril she was in? Was she unaware that the odds were stacked high against her very survival? Did she know what her future held? How short it might be?

"She looked at me and said, 'Gene, I am fully aware that soon, I may not be able to dance. My future is short, and I know that I'm not long for this world. Why would I let what hasn't happened yet cut short my potential in this moment?'

"She looked down the ravine at my wife's crumpled car. She said, 'Life can go by in the blink of an eye. Every moment counts. Today, you are creating both your past and your future. What you do today will tomorrow be your past. Just like what you do today will also determine your tomorrow.

"'You probably see me as not having much of a future. I see myself enjoying the fresh air of today, this breath, and my next. If I spent what time I have today fearing what might come tomorrow, I'd miss out on every precious moment of life that I do have.

"'Moments like this, where I get to meet nice people like you. Want to hear another song? What would you like to hear?'

"I said, 'You pick.' She closed her eyes, and when she opened her mouth, her words took my breath away. She sang the very song from our wedding. My wife's favorite song. I couldn't hold back the tears. She grabbed my hand and squeezed tight.'

Abe wasn't able to hold back tears of his own. He asked, "What was the song?"

"'Earth Angel' . . . the Penguins. She belted it out. This little girl was a miracle that showed up in my life. Impossible that she was anything other than an earth angel herself.

"When she finished the song, she gave me a big hug. I wept openly. She whispered again that everything was going to be all right. She pulled back, looked into my eyes and said, 'They're home. Remember who walks with you. You're never alone.'

"She walked on down the road, turned, waved, and flashed a giant smile at me. I waved back and watched her till she went around the corner. She touched my heart. I took the gun from my pocket, opened the cylinder and dumped the bullets out. I put it back in my pocket. Said a silent prayer of thanks.

"I got in my car and drove home. I'm not going to tell you that it was easy. Or that I never had sorrow again. But Abe, I can tell you this—I never felt alone again. I knew that I had a purpose to be here.

"And that little girl was right—this moment is all we have. Ever. The here and now represents your present, becomes your past, and determines your future. Don't squander what you've been richly blessed with."

Abe put up a hand, "Wait. What I'm blessed with? I have nothing."

"You've heard nothing then. If you think for a minute that you have nothing, then you don't. All the while you have a life and breath in your body. You have an eternal soul. You have a loving wife with a child on the way. You have skills to communicate. You have freedom—freedom to choose what you will do with the rest of your life.

"If you can't see what you have in abundance, then you are doomed to live a life in the bottom of that canyon, even though you've been shown the path to the peak. Abraham, look inside yourself. Remember the lessons you've learned today.

"This life is about serving others. You are not here to get, but to give. If you focus only on yourself, you'll always feel empty. Less than complete. It's when you truly open your heart to a life of service, that's when you'll know the joy of a well-lived life. An abundant life waits for you."

Gene reached out his hand. Abe took it.

"I must go now. Abraham, you have a choice. Choose to live in this moment. Not for the moment, but in this moment. Choose to live, my friend."

Gene opened his door, and a gust of cold wind ripped through the car. Snow was blowing in. He bent down, tipped his red fedora, smiled, and said, "You're not stuck."

He left the door open and faded away in the blinding snow.

Abe was confused. Just a second ago it had been a bright, cloudless day. Now the cold was biting his skin. Snow was piling up in the passenger seat where Gene had just been sitting.

Abe was freezing, unable to move. He tried to unbuckle his seat belt, but couldn't reach. Darkness closed in and overtook his consciousness.

3

Abe heard a beeping sound. Distant at first, then it got closer and louder. He was aware of other sounds, murmuring voices. He couldn't make out any words, but he knew that people were talking nearby. Then total silence.

The next time he heard the beeping, it was loud. Like a horn blasting. He flinched, opened his eyes to a bright light. Too bright. He squeezed them closed. Suddenly aware of a throbbing in his head. He was lying out flat.

Then he felt a hand touching his face. His wife's voice, clearly saying, "Abe. You're alright. I love you. Oh, how I love you."

Abe attempted to open his eyes several more times until they adjusted to the light. There in front of his face was Sam. Beautiful Sam, glowing like an angel. His very own earth angel.

"I'm so sorry," he said, not recognizing his own groggy voice. His throat was killing him.

"Shhhh. Don't speak. Let me get the doctor. Everyone is going to be so happy you're back. Hold on," Sam said as she left his field of view.

Abe tried to look around at his surroundings. Some kind of room with lots of machines, tubes, and big curtains. That's when realization hit home—he was in a hospital.

What happened? How'd I get here?

Then Sam was back, and she brought a doctor. He was in scrubs, dark hair, with a graying beard.

"There he is. How you doing, Abe? You gave us quite a scare, pal," the doctor said as he shone a light into Abe's eyes.

"Where's Gene? Is he OK?" Abe asked in a scratchy voice.

"Let's get you some ice, try and soothe your throat a little," the doctor said.

"What about Gene?" Abe repeated.

The doctor glanced over to Sam, then back at Abe. "Yeah, you asked the EMTs about someone named Gene also. But pal, you were alone. No one else was in the car with you."

Abe closed his eyes, his entire body racked with pain. Sam leaned over and kissed him on the forehead. She whispered, "I love you so much."

"Sam . . . Gene was there. He really was." Abe slipped away into the black once more.

The next thing Abe knew, he felt the earth moving beneath him. He opened his eyes to see the ceiling passing by like a conveyor belt. Bright lights followed by blank ceiling tiles.

"Hey there, buddy," said a voice from his side. "Good to see you awake. We're almost to your new room. You're moving on up, a room with a view."

Abe tried to talk but couldn't make a sound. He watched the ceiling go by, then his world turned and he saw himself pass through a door. He was trying desperately to separate memories from dreams. Had someone said he was in a wreck? No one in the car but him?

What about Gene? Gene had sat there with him while he was stuck on the road. Thoughts raced through his mind forward and back—nothing made sense. There were more voices, bright lights, then nothing.

With his eyes closed, Abe once more heard the beeping sound. This time not far off, but up close. He heard voices, not muffled but clearly. It was Samantha. She was talking with a man, probably the doctor.

"How long before we'll know if there's any . . ." Sam stopped talking midsentence. She'd noticed Abe's eyes were open.

He was looking right at her. The doctor rushed to his side, shone a light in his eyes, left to right. "Abe, there you are. How do you feel? You're in good hands, my friend. Good hands."

Sam sat down on the edge of the bed, took Abe's hand in hers and leaned down low. She kissed his cheek and stroked his hair. "Oh babe. Stay with me . . . stay with me."

That's what Gene said several times. Did Gene know he was in trouble? Impossible, they'd sat there in the car on the side of the road. The sky was bright blue and the sun was out. None of this made any sense.

"I'm here," Abe said, squeezing Sam's hand. "I'm right here."

The doctor adjusted Abe's IV, then excused himself saying he'd be back shortly. "I'll give you two a little space."

Abe never took his eyes off Sam, afraid his world would go dark again. He remembered everything so clearly, but not an accident. He remembered being upset when he left Mr. Westport's office. Then driving towards Hope when the storm started.

"Sam . . . I don't remember an accident. What happened?" he asked in a weak voice.

"Oh, honey, it was bad. You are lucky, real lucky. Are you sure you want to hear about it right now?"

"Yes."

"Well, your car was found tipped up on its side, right at the edge of Devil's Canyon. If your car had gone another foot, you'd have plunged right over the edge. They said it was straight down, nearly a thousand feet." Sam pulled back, covered her face, and wiped at tears flooding from her eyes.

"It's OK, hon, I'm here. I'm not going anywhere." Abe closed his eyes.

"Abe . . . Abe . . ."

"I'm just kidding," Abe said as he popped his eyes open.

"Oh, you, don't do that to me." Sam smiled and took a deep breath, wanting to punch him. But now wasn't the time. There'd be a time and a place where she'd get him back.

"Sam, I don't remember anything about the accident. I saw a man in the road . . ."

"Gene?" Sam asked.

"Yes. Yes, Gene. He was in the road, I slammed on my brakes and spun around. I guess, because the next thing I knew, I was stuck. Right at the edge of the canyon. But I was there, sitting in my seat. Like nothing was wrong, except I couldn't move. I was stuck."

"Abe, you were hanging on for dear life. You were losing blood, and by the time the EMTs got to you, you were hypothermic. The doctor thinks it's the cold that kept you from bleeding to death."

"Wow. I don't get it. Gene sat there with me. He told me the most amazing story . . . about his family. He lost his family, it was so sad." Abe looked up at the ceiling.

"Abe, I don't know what to say. I think you must have hit your head pretty good. You were all alone out there, and that makes me sick. I tried calling you. I didn't know where you were." Sam sat quiet for a moment, then asked, "Why were you going to Hope anyway?"

"I was going for a drive to clear my head. I have a lot to tell you, but Sam, just know that I love you and I'm never going to take off on you again. I'll tell you everything. I promise."

"Abe, I already know we are in financial trouble. You think you've been keeping it from me, but I know. Is that why you were going out to Hope?"

"Yes. I blew the sale with Mr. Westport, and I needed to clear my head. Seemed like at every turn I was running into a wall. Then I guess I practically drove into a wall. I can't believe I was in an accident and didn't even know it.

"I mean, Gene sat there telling me his story. Sam, you won't believe what I learned. Now that I'm saying all this, I realize it sounds crazy. Like I'm crazy. But it wasn't that I hit my head, although it feels like I did. I'm telling you, Gene is real, and he was there with me."

"Like an angel or something?" Sam asked. She clutched at the small gold cross she wore on a thin chain around her neck.

"Yeah, exactly like an angel. An earth angel. Just like his story." Abe smiled even though it hurt. "Sam, I know I can get us out of this mess. Together, we can do it. I'm not scared anymore. I'm not worried about the future, and I've learned from the past. Samantha, I'm here with you right now. You and me." He patted her belly. "And baby makes three. We are together in this moment. I know where we are headed, I'm going to be there for you, and there with you from now on. I've been stuck in the past, when things were easy. I got so focused on the future life I hoped to have, I was ignoring the beautiful life I do have. I promise Sam, you have me. I'm here to stay."

"Oh, Abe, I'm so happy. You know, the reason I was calling was to tell you about the sonogram. I know what we're having."

"You do?" Abe tried to sit up. Pain shot through his legs and abdomen.

"Sit still, don't move." Sam rubbed his shoulders. "Yes, I know. Do you want to know?"

"Yes, I do. But why didn't you tell me you were going in for the ultrasound?"

Sam looked down at the floor, "I did, Abe. You weren't listening and were too focused on your business to hear me."

Abe remembered to be present in this moment. "OK, tell me. I want to know."

~~The End~~ **A New Beginning**

P.S.

Several months after the accident, Abe and Samantha took a lazy trip to Hope. Driving past the very corner that changed their lives, Abe slowed down, and stole a quick peek into the canyon below.

He was long removed from the mindset that had allowed him to wish for having slipped over the edge. Abe was loving his life, his wife, and their greatest joy of all, a baby girl named Gabrielle.

They ate lunch at their favorite café overlooking the harbor. Sam wanted to go do a little shopping afterwards, so Abe agreed to stroll the boardwalk with the baby. With luck she'd drift off into her afternoon nap.

A new bookshop had opened a few doors down from the café. Abe kissed Sam and they agreed to meet in an hour.

He pushed the stroller down the boardwalk with a sense of pride he'd never known in his life. Sales were going incredibly well, although the economy hadn't changed. He had changed, though. He showed up to serve. He lived in the present moment at every step of life and work.

He walked through the door to the bookstore. It had the smell of every good used-book store you've ever been in. A scent that held the best of yesterday, and the promise of tomorrow.

Abe smiled at the old man behind the counter. He was busy reading a Lee Child paperback. Lost in the story, he'd barely noticed Abe and little Gabby come in.

Abe wandered through the tall stacks filled with books without any recognizable order. Cookbooks were next to books on house building that were next to books on learning to speak French in thirty days or less.

A book caught Abe's eye on the top shelf farthest from the front door. He wasn't sure what made him curious. But he had to see it. The green spine was not unlike any other old book in the store, but something drew him to it. He parked Gabrielle nearby, then tugged a step stool over into position. He pulled the book down and took a seat in the leather chair in the corner. Sneaking a peek at the baby confirmed she'd begun her nap. Right on schedule.

The title of the book was worn off the spine, and there was nothing on the front or back. Abe carefully opened to the title page.

Born to Live ... On Purpose!
(Published 1947)
by Eugene Duncan
Page 1.

This is a manual for living a purpose-driven life. Learn from your past, look to the future, and live in the present.

Printed in the United States
By Bookmasters